HALL JOHNSON: Thirty Spirituals

for High Voice and Piano

To access companion recorded accompaniments
online, visit:
www.halleonard.com/mylibrary
Enter Code
"4337-4395-1982-4225"

ED 4354

ISBN-13: 978-1-4234-1591-6
ISBN-10: 1-4234-1591-4

DISTRIBUTED BY

HAL•LEONARD®

7777 W. BLUEMOUND RD. P.O. BOX 13819 MILWAUKEE, WI 53213

Visit Hal Leonard Online at
www.halleonard.com

Contact us:
Hal Leonard
7777 West Bluemound Road
Milwaukee, WI 53213
Email: info@halleonard.com

In Europe, contact:
Hal Leonard Europe Limited
42 Wigmore Street
Marylebone, London, W1U 2RN
Email: info@halleonardeurope.com

In Australia, contact:
Hal Leonard Australia Pty. Ltd.
4 Lentara Court
Cheltenham, Victoria, 3192 Australia
Email: info@halleonard.com.au

HALL JOHNSON

(1888–1970)

Hall Johnson was an important figure in bringing the spiritual to prominence as American art music. He was born on March 12, 1888 in Athens, Georgia, the son of a Methodist minister. As a young child, Johnson heard spirituals sung by his mother and grandmother, both of whom were former slaves. After hearing a violin recital by Joseph Henry Douglas (the grandson of Frederick Douglas), Johnson was determined to play the violin. He received one as a gift when he was 14, and taught himself to play from a self-instruction guide. He attended Atlanta University, Allen University (Columbia, SC), eventually earning his Bachelor of Arts degree from the University of Pennsylvania in 1910. He furthered his studies later in life at the Juilliard School and the University of Southern California.

Johnson moved to New York City in 1914 where he began his musical career as a violinist and violist. He played violin in various dance orchestras and in the pit for Broadway musicals. In 1923 he joined the Negro String Quartet as a violist. This group found acclaim for their performances of contemporary African-American composers, as well as standard European repertoire. In 1925 Johnson turned to choral conducting when he founded the Hall Johnson Choir. This small ensemble of eight singers went on to perform and record for over three decades under Johnson's leadership. Johnson either composed or arranged all of the music for the ensemble. The choir appeared in several stage and film productions including *The Green Pastures* and *Lost Horizon*. In 1951 the group was invited by the U.S. State Department to represent the United States at the International Festival of Fine Arts in West Berlin.

Johnson flourished as a composer and arranger. He composed a folk opera, *Run Little Chillun*, in 1933, which enjoyed a four month Broadway run in the midst of the Great Depression. Other major works include his cantata *Son of Man* (1946) and an operetta *Fi-Yer* (1959). Johnson also coached hundreds of musicians during his career, including Marian Anderson, Harry Belafonte, and Shirley Verett.

Hall Johnson is best known today for his arrangements of spirituals, either for solo voice and piano or chorus. During his lifetime, Johnson published *The Green Pastures Spirituals* in 1930 and *Thirty Negro Spirituals* in 1949; this publication, *Thirty Spirituals*, is a new edition of *Thirty Negro Spirituals*. He was a passionate advocate of the spiritual as an art form, and published an essay in 1965 entitled "Notes on the Negro Spiritual" in which he explained the significance of the spiritual as American music. Many of Johnson's specific thoughts on spirituals and their performance are contained in his preface beginning on page four.

Hall Johnson died on April 30, 1970 after fire swept through his New York apartment. He is remembered as a tireless champion of the spiritual, and his legacy lives on through performances of his work by countless singers over past decades, and for many more decades to come.

Contents

PAGE   **TITLE**

The price of this publication includes access to companion recorded accompaniments online, for download or streaming, using the unique code found on the title page. Visit **www.halleonard.com/mylibrary** and enter the code.

Preface

from the original edition

For the past 40 years the Negro Spiritual has been steadily gaining favor in the church, the concert-hall, the theater, the sound-films, the home, and on the radio—in fact wherever good music is heard and appreciated. The present volume is offered in the hope of serving a two-fold purpose: (1.) To bring to music-lovers in general a collection of familiar and unfamiliar spirituals in arrangements interesting but not difficult; (2.) To furnish program suggestions to concert singers in search of unhackneyed material of this sort. The division of the contents according to tempo and style will facilitate the selection of groups showing both contrast and variety.

The Negro spiritual is a distinct type of music which resembles no other and therefore requires special treatment in performance. The singer who has no first-hand acquaintance with the authentic racial style should have, for the best results, either an intelligent model or a coach who is thoroughly familiar with this music at its source. As this is not always convenient, a few suggestions from one who has made a life-long study of Negro folk song may be welcomed by those having a more than superficial interest in the subject.

THE MUSIC

General Character

The main characteristic of these songs is simplicity. Avoid exaggerations for spurious "racial effects" in both words and music. Sing the words clearly *in your own natural voice*. Although derived from a unique source, these are religious songs for everybody, not "character pieces" requiring a special voice-quality.

Tempo, Rhythm, and Accent

Once the tempo of a particular song is established, avoid any changes. Primitive Negro singing was always accompanied by bodily motion of some sort which created a steady pulsation throughout the performance, no matter how slow the tempo. This rule of inflexible "beat" has, however, two exceptions: (1.) A very few "question and answer" songs, where the change of tempo is deliberate and distinct (see "Religion Is a Fortune," page 94); (2.) Occasionally, in the slower songs, a fermata or pause may occur at an important point (see "Let de Heb'n-light Shine on Me," page 76). The occasional final rallentando (for a broad finish) is a concession to "concert effect" only and would never occur in genuine folk-singing. A good rule is this: vary the dynamics (pp-ff) according to taste, but vary the tempo only when such a definite change is called for by the music itself.

Another concession to the concert soloist is the piano accompaniment. These songs were originally sung *a cappella*, and there was no audience—everybody was singing. For concert solo purposes, however, the instrumental background is necessary. It not only supplies the harmonies but steadies the tempo and points up the rhythms. In the more primitive performances the tempo was stabilized by the "patting" of many feet, and the rhythm clarified by accenting the proper syllables. But, even with the presence of the piano, this important problem of tempo and rhythm is still the *responsibility of the singer* and must be carefully worked out so as to communicate the impression of life and motion inherent in these songs. This is achieved simply by a slight but noticeable accent on the strong-beat syllables of each measure without bodily motion of any sort on the part of the singer. A little study will show that the livelier songs require fewer but more vigorous accents to the measure, while the slower tunes need more frequent emphases, but lighter in weight. Syncopated figures have the stress on the longest syllable.

THE WORDS

The texts of most of these songs are, naturally enough, in the older Negro dialect. The racial qualities should be neither unduly exaggerated in the hope of being more entertaining nor, still worse, "purified" into correct English—for any reason whatever. Either process would utterly spoil the artistic integrity of the performance.

It should be observed that dialect forms do not necessarily arise from ignorance of the correct pronunciation. Sometimes they are deliberately chosen in order to avoid harsh or difficult sounds, or to render the word more serviceable for the immediate occasion. Especially in the Negro folk song, the word is *always* made adjustable to the rhythm of the music. Consequently this altered word-form may vary all the way from the correct English pronunciation to the most extreme contractions of the dialect. In this collection a careful attempt has been made to spell the words as they should sound—which is not always possible. Here are examples of some of the most familiar alterations:

Heaven—Hev'n—Heb'm—Heb'n—or just He'm   For—fŭh or f'
Children—chil-dun—child'n—chillum   To—tŭh or t'
There—dere—dey or day   My—ma—mŭh or m'

In a strongly accented or loud and long syllable, the short "i" is always sung like a short "e." For example, in "Po' Mo'ner Got a Home at Las'" (page 49), the words "mo'nin'," "seekin'," and "preachin'" are sung as "mo'nen," "seeken," and "preachen." The most common example is the alteration of "if" into "eff."

The final syllables of words like "people" and "trouble" become darker and heavier, and sound like the "ul" in the word "cull."

The English "the," "this," and "that" are sometimes preferred to the dialect "de," "dis," and "dat."

"De" (like "the") is *always* pronounced "dee" before vowels and "dŭh" before consonants.

Initial letters are sometimes omitted for the sake of smoother legato, and some final letters, which would ordinarily be dropped, are not only sounded but even emphasized in order to accent the following syllable.

Finally, there is one all-important consideration—the right *mental* attitude on the part of the singer. Without this factor, the most careful observance of the preceding suggestions will result only in an empty and meaningless performance. True enough, this music was transmitted to us through humble channels, but its source is that of all great art everywhere—the unquenchable, divinely human longing for a perfect realization of life. It traverses every shade of emotion without spilling over in any direction. Its most tragic utterances are without pessimism, and its lightest, brightest moments have nothing to do with frivolity. In its darkest expressions there is always a hope, and in its gayest measures a constant reminder. Born out of the heart-cries of a captive people who did not forget how to laugh, this music covers an amazing range of mood. Nevertheless, it is *always* serious music and should be performed seriously, in the spirit of its original conception.

Quite often the swinging syncopations of the rhythms and the occasional quaint humor of the words carry a smile which no modern audience can possibly resist. However, the enjoyment of this audience will be greatly deepened and sweetened if the singer stays in the spirit of the song and leaves the smile to the listeners. Too many conscientious (and otherwise intelligent) singers deliberately "play these songs for comedy," hoping to make the audience laugh at something that has never been and never will be funny. To discerning and enlightened minds, these artists succeed only in demeaning their art, which then necessarily suffers by comparison with the inner value of the very material it is pretending to illuminate.

On the other hand, in direct proportion as these songs are delivered with simplicity, even with reverence, each song being allowed to speak for itself, the singer will find his audience-reaction more and more gratifying and himself vastly enriched by the experience.

—Hall Johnson
originally published in 1949

MODIFIED ENGLISH TEXTS

for the spirituals

Despite Hall Johnson's directions about diction (see "The Words" section of his original preface), some contemporary singers may not be comfortable with all the dialect, preserved in the musical score as prepared by Johnson. We present modified standard English below, without grammatical changes. Singers may choose to combine dialect with standard English in performance in a modern sensibility, while still following the spirit of Johnson's intentions, and a casual, spoken, folk diction approach. We retained the dropped "g" in words in –ing endings. Particularly note from Johnson's preface the instruction to sing "to" as tŭh or t'. The final "d" in the word "and" should be dropped in folk diction. The final "t" is also probably dropping in a word such as "don't." There are various versions of the lyrics of these spirituals which may be encountered in other published sources. (One may even encounter significant melodic differences in various spiritual editions.) Johnson made choices in his settings, which we retain.

BELSHAZZA' HAD A FEAS'
(BELSHAZZAR HAD A FEAST)
VERSE 1
Belshazzar had a feast and
there's a hand writin' on the wall.
Come and read it and
tell me what it say there
Hand writin' on the wall.

VERSE 2
"Mene, mene, tekel,"*
said the hand writin' on the wall.
Come and read it and
tell me what it say there
Hand writin' on the wall.

VERSE 3
Terrestrial and celestial,
a hand writin' on the wall.
Come and read it and
tell me what it say there
Hand writin' on the wall.

VERSE 4
Sodom and Gomorra',
there's a hand writin' on the wall.
Come and read it and
tell me what it say there
Hand writin' on the wall.

VERSE 5
Cherubim and Seraphim,
a hand writin' on the wall.
Come and read it and
tell me what it say there
Hand writin' on the wall.

---

* These words were written by a mysterious hand on the wall of Belshazzar's palace. Daniel interprets them as predicting the downfall of the king and his dynasty.

VERSE 6
Holy, holy, holy,
there's a hand writin' on the wall.
Come and read it and
tell me what it say there
Hand writin' on the wall.

DAT SUITS ME
(THAT SUITS ME)
VERSES 1 and 5
Oh, come on, Elder,
let's go 'round the wall,
That suits me.
I don't want to stumble
and I don't want to fall,
That suits me.

VERSE 2
Oh, come on, Sister,
won't you help me to sing?
That suits me.
This feelin' in my bosom
is a happy thing,
That suits me.

VERSE 3
Oh, you can weep like a willow,
you can mourn like a dove,
That suits me.
But if you want to get to Heaven
you got to go with love,
That suits me.

VERSE 4
Oh, when I die, Lord,
I want to die right,
That suits me.
I want to march up in the Kingdom
all dressed in white,
That suits me.

DONE WRITTEN DOWN MY NAME
REFRAIN
Oh, members, rise, oh rise,
And don't you be ashamed.
Oh, Jesus Christ, the Lamb of God,
Done written down my name.

VERSE 1
In the Kingdom,
written down my name.
In the Lamb's book,
written down my name.

VERSE 2
On the mountain,
written down my name.
In the valley,
written down my name.
On the highway,
written down my name.
In the hedges,
written down my name.

EV'RY TIME I FEEL DE SPIRIT
REFRAIN
Ev'ry time I feel the spirit
Movin' in my heart, I will pray.

VERSE 1
On the mountain my Lord spoke,
Out of His mouth came fire and smoke.
In the valley, on my knees,
Ask' my Lord have mercy, please.

VERSE 2
Jordan river chilly and cold,
Chills the body but not the soul.
All around me look so shine,
Ask' my Lord if all was mine.

VERSE 3
Ain't but one train on this track,
Runs to Heaven and runs right back.
Saint Peter waitin' at the gate
Says, "Come on sinner, don't be late."

GLORY HALLELUJAH
TO DE NEW-BORN KING
VERSE 1
Tell me who do you call the Wonderful Counsellor?
Oh, Glory Hallelujah to the new-born King!
Well, I call Jesus the Wonderful Counsellor.
Oh, Glory Hallelujah to the new-born King.

VERSE 2
Just follow the Star and you'll find the Baby,
Oh, Glory Hallelujah to the new-born King.
You'll find Him in Bethlehem wrapped in the manger,
Oh, Glory Hallelujah to the new-born King.

VERSE 3
Cryin' "Peace on earth, good-will to your neighbor."
Oh, Glory Hallelujah to the new-born King.
Didn't Jesus say ev'ry man is your neighbor?
Oh, Glory Hallelujah to the new-born King!

GOSPEL TRAIN
VERSE 1
The gospel train is a-comin',
I hear it just at hand.
I hear the car-wheels movin',
And a-rumblin' through the land.

REFRAIN and ENDING
Oh, get on board, little children,
There's room for many-a more.

VERSE 2
I hear the bell and whistle,
She's comin' round the curve.
She's playin' all her steam and pow'r
And strainin' ev'ry nerve.

VERSE 3
The fare is cheap and all can go,
The rich and poor are there.
No second class on board this train,
No diff'rence in the fare.

VERSE 4
She's nearin' now the station,
Oh, sinner, don't be vain,
But come and get your ticket
And be ready for this train.

GREATE DAY!

GREAT DAY!

REFRAIN
Oh, Great Day! The righteous marchin'.
Great Day! God's gone to build up Zion's wall.

VERSE 1
Chariot moved on the mountain top,
God's gone to build up Zion's wall.
My Lord spoke and the chariot stopped.
God's gone to build up Zion's wall.

VERSE 2
This is the year of Jubilee,
God's gone to build up Zion's wall.
When my Lord set His people free,
God's gone to build up Zion's wall.

VERSE 3
When I was a mourner just like you,
God's gone to build up Zion's wall.
I prayed and prayed till I come through,
God's gone to build up Zion's wall.

VERSE 4
We want no cowards in our band,
God's gone to build up Zion's wall.
We call for valiant-hearted men,
God's gone to build up Zion's wall.

HOW LONG TRAIN BEEN GONE?

VERSE 1
Oh, how many members gone?
Won't be back till Judgment day,
Done took that train and gone.
Won't be back till Judgment Day.

REFRAIN
Oh, how long train been gone?
Won't be back till Judgment Day.

VERSE 2
Oh, the old class-leader's gone,
Won't be back till Judgment Day,
Done took that train and gone.
Won't be back till Judgment Day.

VERSE 3
Oh, all them disciples gone,
Won't be back till Judgment Day,
Done took that train and gone.
Won't be back till Judgment Day.

I COULDN' HEAR NOBODY PRAY

REFRAIN
Lord, I couldn't hear nobody pray.
Oh, way down yonder by myself,
And I couldn't hear nobody pray.

VERSE 1
In the valley,
On my knees,
With my burden,
And my Saviour,
And I couldn't hear nobody pray.

VERSE 2
Chilly waters,
In the Jordan,
Crossin' over,
Into Canaan,
And I couldn't hear nobody pray.

VERSE 3
Hallelujah!
Trouble's over,
In the Kingdom,
With my Jesus,
And I couldn't hear nobody pray.

KEEP A-INCHIN' ALONG

REFRAIN
Keep a-inchin' along;
Jesus will come by and by.
Keep a-inchin' along
like a poor inchworm;
Jesus will come by and by.

VERSE 1
It was inch by inch that I sought the Lord,
Jesus will come by and by.
It was inch by inch that He saved my soul,
Jesus will come by and by.
(Oh, children)

VERSE 2
We'll inch and inch and inch along,
Jesus will come by and by.
And inch by inch till we get home,
Jesus will come by and by.
(Hallelujah)

9

LEANIN' ON DAT LAMB
(LEANIN' ON THAT LAMB)
VERSE 1
Oh, longtime mourner,
won't you come out the wilderness?
Leanin' on that Lamb.

REFRAIN
I'm leanin' on that Lamb of God
That takes away the sins of the world.

VERSE 2
Oh, long-tongue liar,
won't you come out the wilderness?
Leanin' on that Lamb.

VERSE 3
Oh, back-bitin' Christian,
won't you come out the wilderness?
Leanin' on that Lamb.

LET DE HEB'N-LIGHT SHINE ON ME
(LET THE HEAV'N-LIGHT SHINE ON ME)
VERSE 1
Let the Heav'n-light shine on me.
For low is the way
to the upper bright world,
Let the Heav'n-light shine on me.

VERSE 2
Oh, brother, you must bow so low.
For low is the way
to the upper bright world,
Let the Heav'n-light shine on me.

MARY HAD A BABY
VERSES 1, 3, 6
Mary had a baby,
The people keep a-comin'
and the train done gone.

VERSE 2
Star keep a-shinin',
Movin' in the elements,
Stood above the stable,
The people keep a-comin'
and the train done gone.

VERSE 4
Where did she lay him?
Laid him in the manger,
Wrapped in the swaddlin',
The people keep a-comin'
and the train done gone.

VERSE 5
What did she name him?
Named him King Jesus,
Wonderful Counsellor,
The people keep a-comin'
and the train done gone.

MY LORD, WHAT A MORNIN'
REFRAIN
My Lord, what a mornin'!
Oh, my Lord, what a mornin'
When the stars begin to fall.

VERSE 1
You'll hear the trumpet sound
To wake the nations underground,
Lookin' to my God's right hand
When the stars begin to fall.

VERSE 2
You'll hear the singers moan
To see the righteous marchin' home,
Lookin' to my God's right hand
When the stars begin to fall.

OH, FREEDOM
VERSES 1 and 5
Oh, Freedom over me.
And before I'd be a slave
I'd be buried in my grave
And go home to my Lord and be free.

VERSE 2
No more weepin' over me.
And before I'd be a slave
I'd be buried in my grave
And go home to my Lord and be free.

VERSE 3
Same old sunshine over me.
And before I'd be a slave
I'd be buried in my grave
And go home to my Lord and be free.

VERSE 4
God Almighty over me.
And before I'd be a slave
I'd be buried in my grave
And go home to my Lord and be free.

OH, GRAVEYARD
VERSE 1
Oh, graveyard, oh, graveyard,
I'm walkin' through the graveyard,
Lay this body down.

VERSE 2
I know moonlight, I know starlight,
I'm walkin' through the starlight,
Lay this body down.

VERSE 3
Oh, my soul, oh, your soul,
I'm walkin' through the graveyard,
Lay this body down.

OVER YONDER
VERSE 1
I got a sister over yonder,
On the other shore.
By and by I'm goin' to see her,
On the other shore.

VERSE 2
I got a brother over yonder,
On the other shore.
By and by I'm goin' to see him,
On the other shore.

VERSE 3
I got a mother over yonder,
On the other shore.
By and by I'm goin' to see her,
On the other shore.

PO' MO'NER GOT A HOME AT LAS'
(POOR MOURNER GOT A HOME AT LAST)
REFRAIN
Oh, no harm, Tell Brother 'Lijah. [Elijah]
Mourner got a home at last.

VERSE 1
Oh, mourner,
Ain't you tired of mournin'?
Fall down on-a your knees
and-a join the band-a with the angels.

VERSE 2
Oh, seeker,
Ain't you tired of seekin'?
Fall down on-a your knees
and-a join the band-a with the angels.

VERSE 3
Oh, preacher,
Ain't you tired of preachin'?
Fall down on-a your knees
and-a join the band-a with the angels.

CODA
My Lord.
Poor mourner got a home at last.

PRAYER IS DE KEY
REFRAIN
Oh, prayer is the key, bretheren,
Prayer is the key, Lord,
Unlock the Heaven-door for me.

VERSE 1
On your knees, down on your knees,
Unlock the Heaven-door for me.
Seek and find them golden keys,
Unlock the Heaven-door for me.

VERSE 2
Bend your knees right smooth with the ground,
Unlock the Heaven-door for me.
Pray to the Lord for to turn you 'round,
Unlock the Heaven-door for me.

RELIGION IS A FORTUNE
VERSE 1
Oh, religion is a fortune,
I really do believe,
Where Sabbath has no end.
Where you been poor mourner,
Oh, where you been so long?
I been-a way down in the valley for to pray,
And I ain't done prayin' yet.

VERSE 2
Gone to set down in the Kingdom,
I really do believe,
Where Sabbath has no end.
Where you been young convert,
Oh, where you been so long?
I been-a way down in the valley for to pray,
And I ain't done prayin' yet.

VERSE 3
Gone to see my Sister Mary,
I really do believe,
Where Sabbath has no end.
Where you been back-slider,
Oh, where you been so long?
I been-a way down in the valley for to pray,
And I ain't done prayin' yet.

VERSE 4
Gone to see my Master Jesus,
I really do believe,
Where Sabbath has no end.

RIDE ON, JESUS!
REFRAIN
Oh, ride on, Jesus!
Ride on, conquerin' King,
Lord, I want to go to Heaven in the mornin'.

VERSE 1
If you see my sister, Oh, yes!
Won't you tell her for me, Oh, yes!
Lord, I want to go to Heaven in the mornin'.

VERSE 2
If you see my brother, Oh, yes!
Won't you tell him for me, Oh, yes!
Lord, I want to go to Heaven in the mornin'.

VERSE 3
If you see my mother, Oh, yes!
Won't you tell her for me, Oh, yes!
Lord, I want to go to Heaven in the mornin'.

SCANDALIZE' MY NAME
VERSE 1
Well, I met my sister the other day,
Give her my right hand,
Just as soon as every my back was turned
she took and scandalized my name.
Do you call that a sister? No! No!
Scandalized my name.

VERSE 2
Well, I met my brother the other day,
Give him my right hand,
Just as soon as every my back was turned
he took and scandalized my name.
Do you call that a brother? No! No!
Scandalized my name.

VERSE 3
Well, I met my preacher the other day,
Give him my right hand,
Just as soon as every my back was turned
he took and scandalized my name.
Do you call that religion? No! No!
Scandalized my name!

SINNER-MAN SO HARD TO BELIEVE
VERSES 1 and 5
Ain't that a pity, Lord,
Ain't that a shame!
Sin and a shame!
Sinner-man so hard to believe.

VERSE 2
Dives was a rich man,
Laz'rus was poor,
Sinner-man so hard to believe.

VERSE 3
Laz'rus in a Heaven,
Dives in Hell,
Sinner-man so hard to believe.

VERSE 4
My mother and your mother
both dead and gone,
Sinner-man so hard to believe.

**STAN' STILL, JORDAN
(STAND STILL, JORDAN)**
VERSES 1 and 4
Stand still, Jordan,
Lord, I can't stand still.

VERSE 2
You may bury my body,
But I can't stand still.

VERSE 3
When I feel the Spirit,
Lord, I can't stand still.

**STAN'IN' IN DE NEED OF PRAYER
(STANDIN' IN THE NEED OF PRAYER)**
REFRAIN
It's me, oh Lord,
Standin' in the need of prayer.

VERSE 1
Ain't my brother nor my sister
but it's me, oh, Lord,
Standin' in the need of prayer.

VERSE 2
Ain't my mother nor my father
but it's me, oh, Lord,
Standin' in the need of prayer.

VERSE 3
Ain't my deacon nor my elder
but it's me, oh, Lord,
Standin' in the need of prayer.

SWING LOW, SWEET CHARIOT!
REFRAIN
Oh, swing low, sweet chariot,
Comin' for to carry me home.

VERSE 1
I looked over Jordan and what did I see,
Comin' for to carry me home?
A band of angels comin' after me,
Comin' for to carry me home.

VERSE 2
If you get there before I do,
Comin' for to carry me home.
Tell all my friends I'm a-comin', too.
Comin' for to carry me home.

THERE IS A BALM IN GILEAD
REFRAIN
There is a balm in Gilead
To make the wounded whole.
There is a balm in Gilead
To heal the sin-sick soul.

VERSE 1
Sometimes I feel discouraged
And think my work's in vain,
But then the Holy Spirit
revives my soul again.

VERSE 2
If you can't preach like Peter,
If you can't pray like Paul,
Go home and tell your neighbor
He died to save us all.

THIS IS DE HEALIN' WATER
REFRAIN
Oh, this is the healin' water.
Be baptized.
It's flowin' from the fountain.
Be baptized.

VERSE 1
Come along, mourner.
Be baptized.

VERSE 2
Come along, seeker.
Be baptized.

VERSE 3
Come along, sinner.
Be baptized.

WERE YOU THERE?
VERSE 1
Were you there when they crucified my Lord?
Oh, sometimes it causes me to tremble.
Were you there when they crucified my Lord?

VERSE 2
Were you there when they nailed Him to the tree?
Oh, sometimes it causes me to tremble.
Were you there when they nailed Him to the tree?

VERSE 3
Were you there when they laid Him in the tomb?
Oh, sometimes it causes me to tremble.
Were you there when they laid Him in the tomb?

VERSE 4
Were you there when they rolled the stone away?
Oh, sometimes it causes me to tremble.
Were you there when they crucified my Lord?

WHEN I LAY MY BURDEN DOWN
VERSES 1 and 8
Oh, Glory, glory! Hallelujah!
When I lay my burden down.

VERSE 2
I'll be leavin' all my troubles,
When I lay my burden down.

VERSE 3
I'll be crossin' over Jordan,
When I lay my burden down.

VERSE 4
I'll be marchin' in the Kingdom,
When I lay my burden down.

VERSE 5
I'll be climbin' Jacob's Ladder,
When I lay my burden down.

VERSE 6
I'll be chatt'rin' with my Jesus,
When I lay my burden down.

VERSE 7
I'll be restin' from my labor,
When I lay my burden down.

MODERATE and RHYTHMIC

Hall Johnson's original introduction for the section

The songs in this group are *moderate* and *steady* in tempo and must have the rhythms quite strongly marked. On each accented beat the consonant must strike the vowel quickly and vigorously, even in the soft passages.

In order to avoid monotony, the singer may (1) vary the dynamics in the verse-lines according to the meaning of the words, and (2) omit occasionally (not always) the recurring choral-response line, leaving this unavoidable repetition to the piano. Whenever this latter device is employed, the "lead-line" may be held over a bit into the "choral-response" of the piano.

For example, in "Ride on, Jesus!" (page 40), the words "Oh, yes," should be sung in the first verse only. Once they are established as an integral part of the song, they may be left to the piano. The singer will then have more time, breath, and attention to devote to the changing verse-lines.

The entire song "How Long Train Been Gone?" (page 32) is a long decrescendo, beginning quite loud and ending very quietly. In the last, soft refrains, the singer may lengthen the word "long," and let the piano "say" "train-a been gone."

The narrative "Belshazza' Had a Feas'" (page 14) is given a mystic quality by the sudden dynamic effects suggested, but only if the "consonant-attacks" are kept sharp and vigorous throughout—even in the pianissimo passages. The words "terrasle an' cellasle" mean "terrestrial and celestial."

"I Couldn' Hear Nobody Pray" (page 16) is more quietly subjective than the other songs in this group, hence it should have a more generous though just as steady tempo. The consonants are still accented, but not quite so sharply. The concluding phrase should be considerably slower and softer. Sustain all the verse-lines as indicated, leaving the response to the piano.

BELSHAZZA' HAD A FEAS'

original key

Arranged by
Hall Johnson

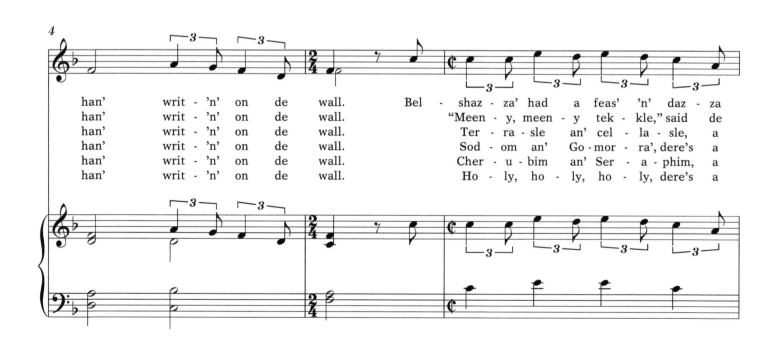

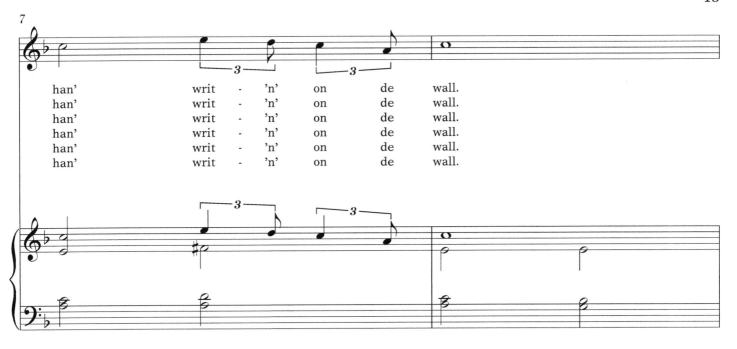

han'   writ - 'n' on de wall.
han'   writ - 'n' on de wall.
han'   writ - 'n' on de wall.
han'   writ - 'n' on de wall.
han'   writ - 'n' on de wall.
han'   writ - 'n' on de wall.

Come   an' read   it 'n' tell me what it say dair,

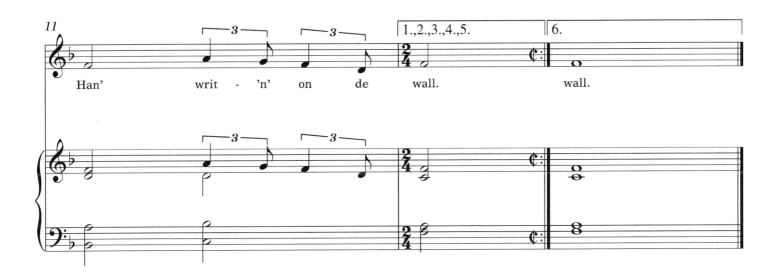

Han'   writ - 'n' on de wall.   wall.

I COULDN' HEAR NOBODY PRAY

original key

Arranged by
Hall Johnson

The musical form of this edition has been slightly adapted from Johnson's original.

Verses

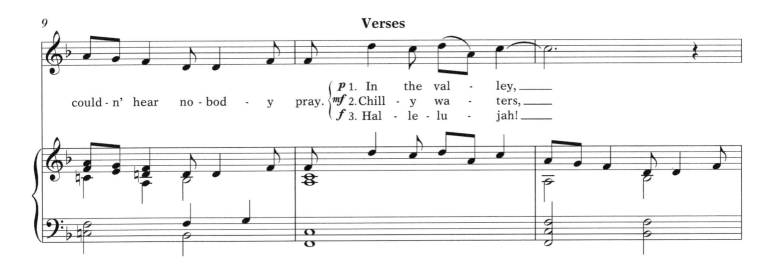

could-n' hear no-bod-y pray.
p 1. In the val - ley, ____
mf 2. Chill - y wa - ters, ____
f 3. Hal - le - lu - jah! ____

On ma knees, ____
In de Jer - don, ____
Trou - ble's o - ver, ____

Wid ma bur - den, ____
Cross - in' o - ver, ____
In de King - dom, ____

____ An' ma Sav - iour, ____
____ In - to Ca - naan, ____
____ Wid ma Je - sus, ____

Oh Lord, _ you know I

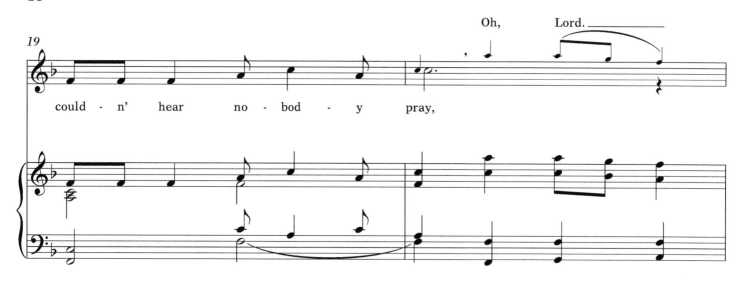

could - n' hear no - bod - y pray,

Could - n' hear no - bod - y pray. Oh, way down yon - der

Slower and softer for end of song

by ___ my - self, An' I could - n' hear no - bod - y pray.

DAT SUITS ME

original key

Arranged by
Hall Johnson

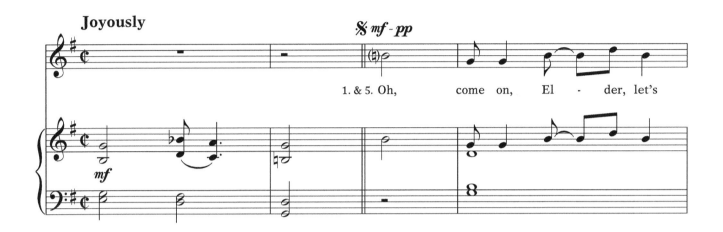

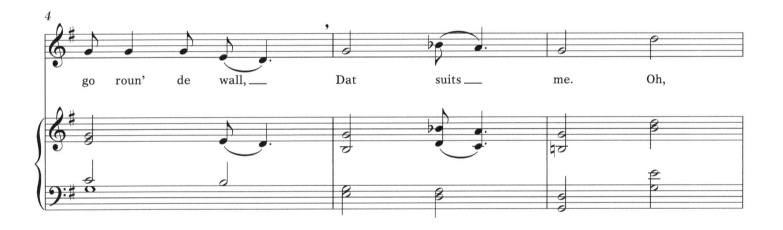

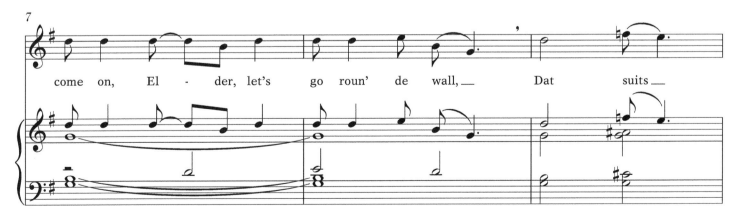

Note: Take new breath *only* before the word "Dat."

me. Oh, come on, El - der, let's go roun' de wall; I

[*rit. last time*]

don' want - er stum - ble an' I don' want - er fall, ___ Dat suits ___

Fine

me. 2. Oh, come on, Sis - ter, won't you help me to sing? ___

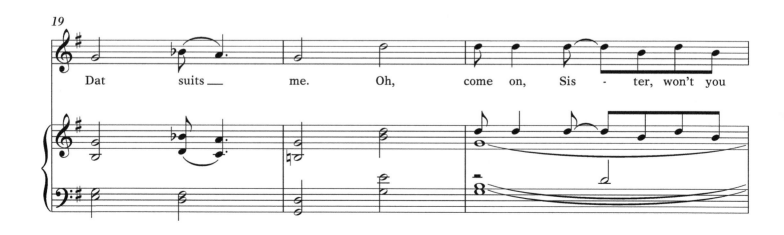

Dat suits ___ me. Oh, come on, Sis - ter, won't you

help me to sing? __ Dat suits __ me. Oh,

come on, Sis - ter, won't you help me to sing? Dis feel-in' in my bo-som is a

hap - py thing, __ Dat suits __ me. 3. Oh, you kin

weep like a wil - ler, you kin mo'n like a dove, __ Dat suits __

want-er die right,____ Dat suits ____ me. Oh,

when I die,____ Lord, I want-er die right,____ Dat suits____

me. Oh, when I die,____ Lord, I want-er die right, I want-er

march up in de King-dom all dressed in white,____ Dat suits____ me.

D.S. al Fine

DONE WRITTEN DOWN MY NAME

original key

Arranged by
Hall Johnson

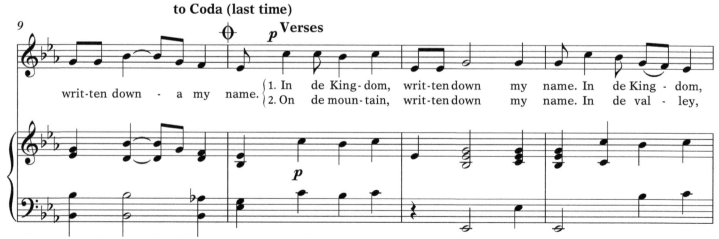

The musical form of this edition has been slightly adapted from Johnson's original.

GREAT DAY!

original key

Arranged by
Hall Johnson

Vigorous March

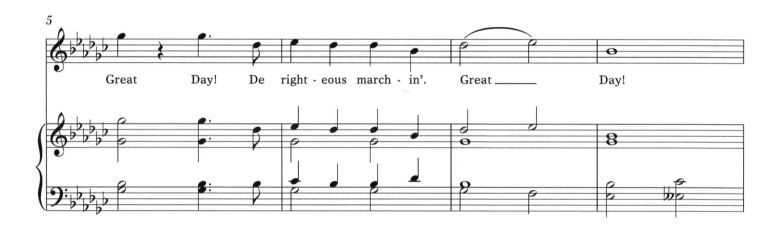

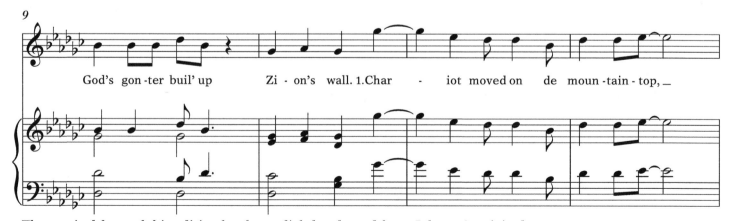

The musical form of this edition has been slightly adapted from Johnson's original.

God's gon-ter buil' up Zi-on's wall. My_____ Lord spoke an' de

char-iot stopped. God's gon-ter buil' up Zi-on's wall. Oh,

Refrain

Great_____ Day! Great Day! De right-eous march-in'.

Great_____ Day! God's gon-ter buil' up Zi-on's wall. 2. Dis

is de year _ of Ju-ber-lee, _ God's gon-ter buil' up Zi-on's wall. When

my Lord set His peo-ple free, _ God's gon-ter buil' up Zi-on's wall. Oh,

Refrain

Great _____ Day! Great Day! De right-eous march - in'.

Great _____ Day! God's gon-ter buil' up Zi-on's wall. 3.When

I was a mo'n-er jus' like you, God's gon-ter buil' up Zi - on's wall. I

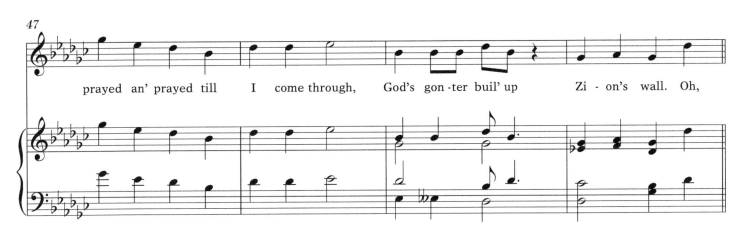

prayed an' prayed till I come through, God's gon-ter buil' up Zi - on's wall. Oh,

Refrain

Great _____ Day! Great Day! De right-eous march-in'.

Great _____ Day! God's gon-ter buil' up Zi - on's wall. 4. We

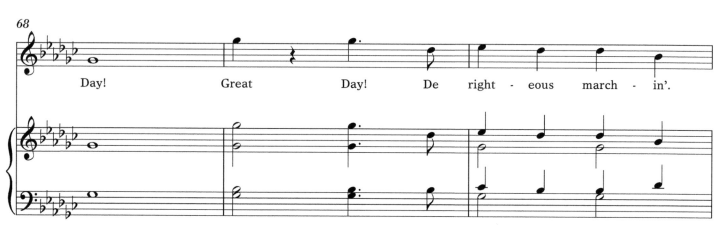

HOW LONG TRAIN BEEN GONE?

original key

Arranged by
Hall Johnson

Stern lament

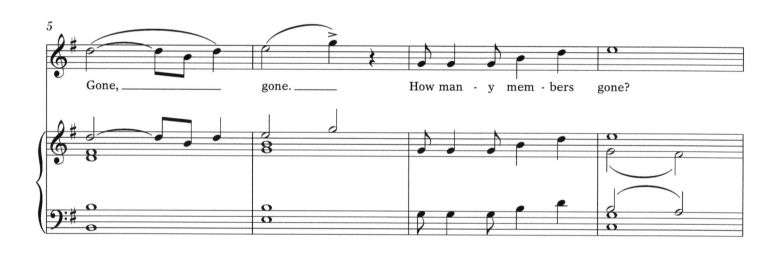

*The repeat is optional on this refrain.

*The repeat is optional on this refrain.

KEEP A-INCHIN' ALONG

original key: A-flat major

Arranged by
Hall Johnson

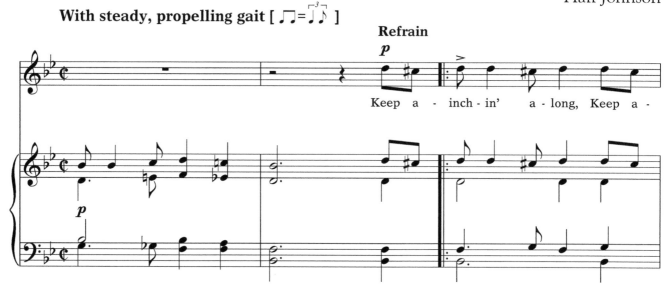

The musical form of this edition has been slightly adapted from Johnson's original.

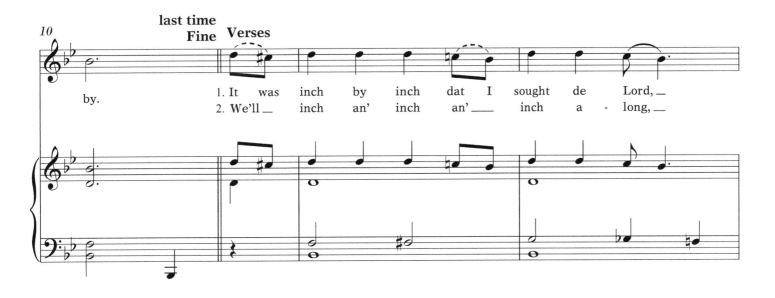

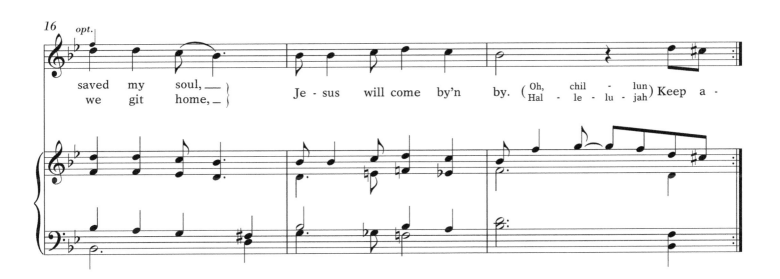

RIDE ON, JESUS!

original key

Arranged by
Hall Johnson

The musical form of this edition has been slightly adapted from Johnson's original.

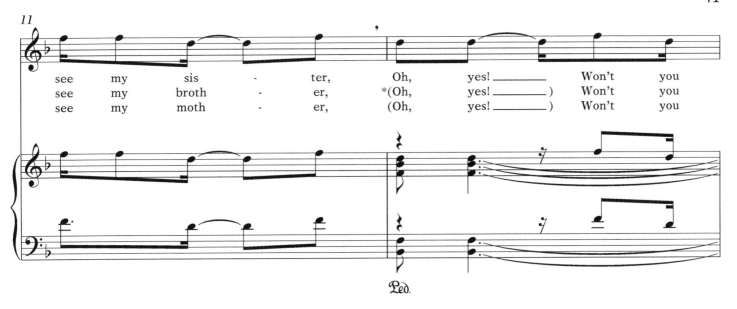

*Johnson suggests this response be sung in the first verse only.

SCANDALIZE' MY NAME

original key: A major

Arranged by
Hall Johnson

The musical form of this edition has been slightly adapted from Johnson's original.

OH, FREEDOM

original key: C major

Arranged by
Hall Johnson

SLOW BUT RHYTHMIC

Hall Johnson's original introduction for the section

"Swing Low, Sweet Chariot!" (page 64) is the most widely known of all the spirituals and for that reason has withstood more mistreatment and more distortions of tempo and style than any of the others. Soloists, quartets, concert orchestras, and swing-bands have each tried to do something "different" with it, but this grand old song still retains its quality of sculptural simplicity combined with an element of majestic elevation for all who will study it with love.

Like all the "vehicle-songs" (about ships, boats, trains, etc.), it must be sung in a steady tempo with inflexible, strongly-accented rhythm. The final refrains may be sung very softly, but not "crooned." Sharp consonants will prevent that.

The word "low" must be sustained up to the quarter-rest, otherwise the effect will be jerky. The word "carry" is reduced to one syllable in order to avoid two smaller notes, but the letter "a" must keep the same sound as in the complete word. Finally, even for a pianissimo finish, the tempo should not be noticeably broadened. A slight lingering on the "h" of the very last "home" will be sufficient.

"There Is a Balm in Gilead" (page 68) should have a more "relaxed" feeling than the other songs in this group. The consonants need not be so percussive nor the tempo so metronomic. In fact, the second note of the slurred words should always have a little extra breadth and, at the end of the verses, a regular pause.

In "Mary Had a Baby" (page 52), omit the response line "Yes Lord," in verse 2, 4, and 5. Sing those words only in the verses beginning with the title.

In "This Is de Healin' Water" (page 72), the consonants must be extra heavy on all beats in order to communicate the "swaying" motion this song must suggest. Notice the deliberate use of the English "this" instead of the dialect form. The "th" gives more prominence to the accented word, and here there is time to say it. The final "d" of "baptized" should be sung very lightly.

LEANIN' ON DAT LAMB

original key

Arranged by
Hall Johnson

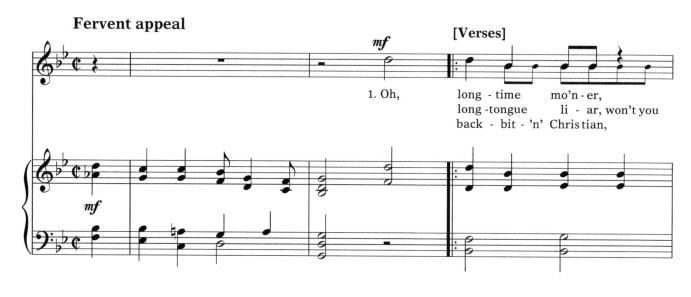

The musical form of this edition has been slightly adapted from Johnson's original.

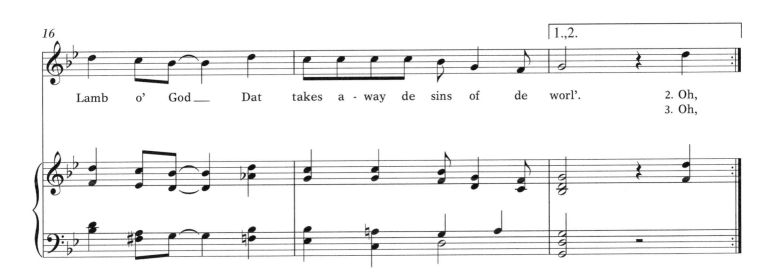

PO' MO'NER GOT A HOME AT LAS'

original key

Arranged by
Hall Johnson

The musical form of this edition has been slightly adapted from Johnson's original.

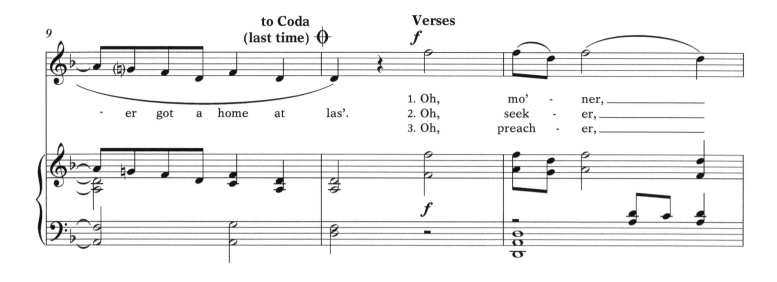

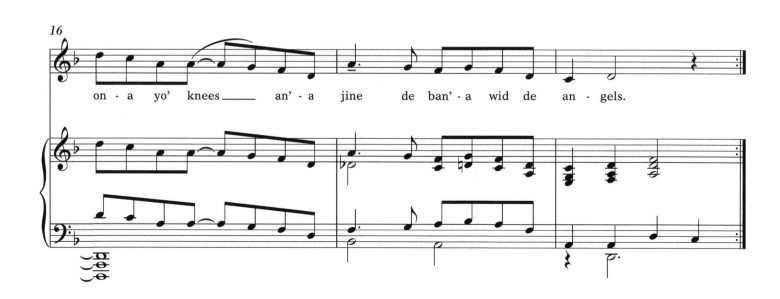

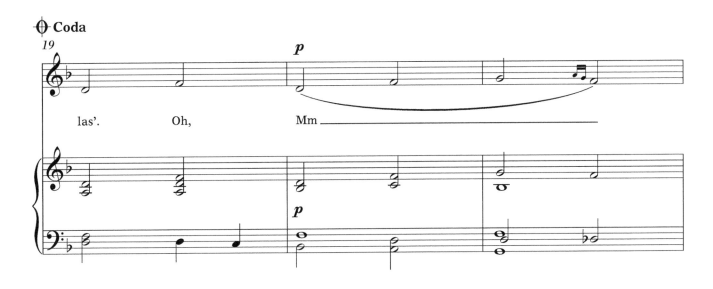

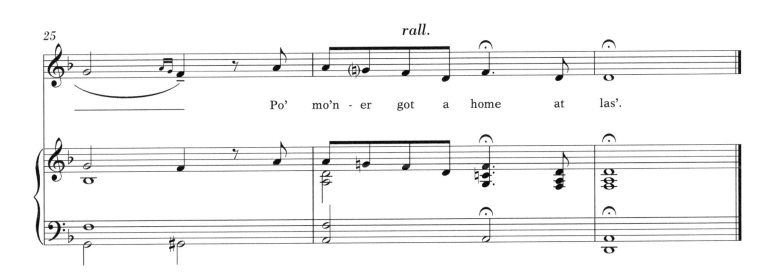

MARY HAD A BABY

Christmas Spiritual

original key

Arranged by
Hall Johnson

Lullaby

*Johnson suggests singing the response "Yes, Lord" only in the verses beginning with the title.

D.S. al Fine

OVER YONDER

original key: F minor

Arranged by
Hall Johnson

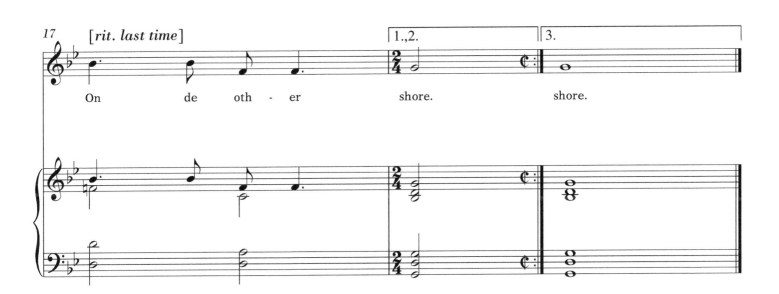

PRAYER IS DE KEY

original key: F major

Arranged by
Hall Johnson

The musical form of this edition has been slightly adapted from Johnson's original.

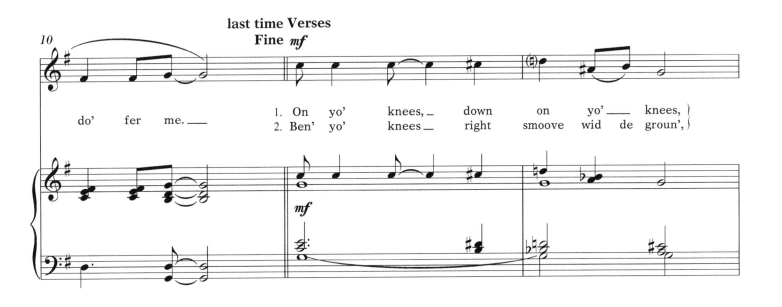

last time Verses
Fine *mf*

do' fer me. ___

1. On yo' knees, ___ down on yo' ___ knees,
2. Ben' yo' knees ___ right smoove wid de groun',

Un-lock de Heav-en - do' fer me. ___

Seek an' fin' ___ dem
Pray to de Lord ___ fer ter

gold - en ___ keys,
turn you ___ 'roun',

Un - lock de Heav-en - do' fer me. ___ Oh, ___

SINNER-MAN SO HARD TO BELIEVE

original key

Arranged by
Hall Johnson

STAN'IN' IN DE NEED OF PRAYER

original key

Arranged by
Hall Johnson

Rocking prayer

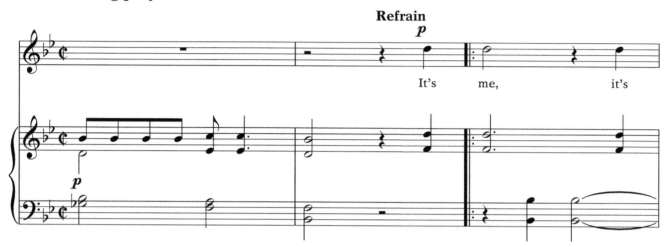

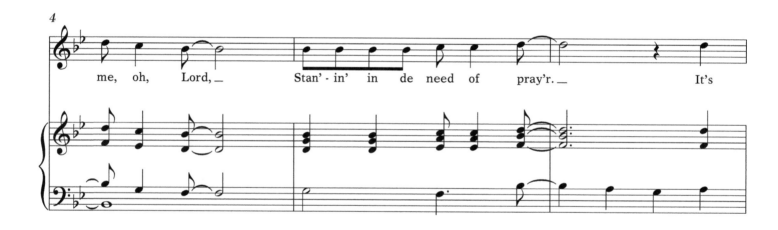

The musical form of this edition has been slightly adapted from Johnson's original.

SWING LOW, SWEET CHARIOT!

original key

Arranged by
Hall Johnson

With accented rhythm

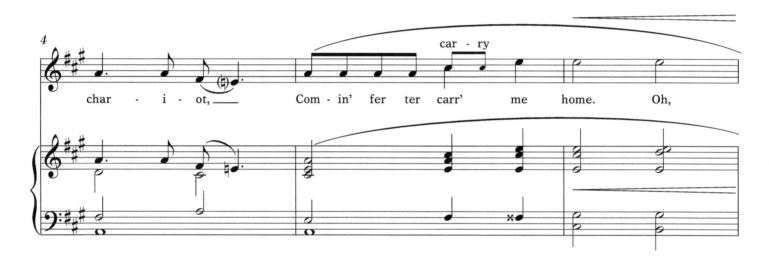

The musical form of this edition has been slightly adapted from Johnson's original.

THERE IS A BALM IN GILEAD

original key

Arranged by
Hall Johnson

Calm and a bit free

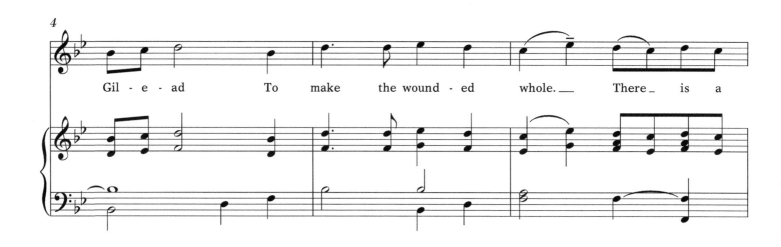

The musical form of this edition has been slightly adapted from Johnson's original.

soul. 1. Some - times I feel dis - cour - aged And

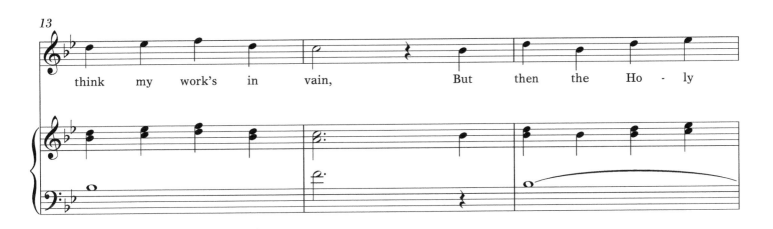

think my work's in vain, But then the Ho - ly

Refrain

Spir - it re - vives my soul a - gain.___ There ___ is a

balm in Gil - e - ad To make the wound - ed

THIS IS DE HEALIN' WATER

original key

Arranged by
Hall Johnson

Accent the "sway"

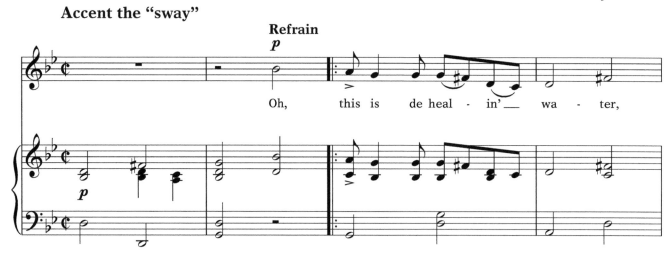

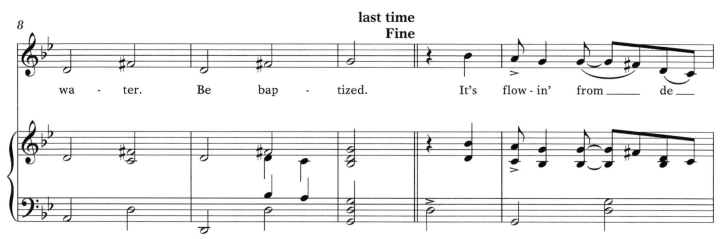

The musical form of this edition has been slightly adapted from Johnson's original.

Verses

SLOW AND QUIET

Hall Johnson's original introduction for the section

In "Were You There?" (page 82), a few suggestions are offered toward securing dynamic variety. However, these should not be overdone. A touch of color may be added to the repeated word "tremble" by slightly suppressing the letter "e" in the first syllable and accenting the surrounding consonants "tr-m." This should be done with the first two only. The third time, the "e" should have its normal length. In all three, however, the "tr" must keep the sound it has in *all* American folksongs, like "ch" in the word "church." A *pure* "tr" is absolutely foreign to this type of music, Negro or otherwise.

Notice how in "Stan' Still, Jordan" (page 84) the verse-line mounts in range and intensity with each repetition. This must not be overlooked. Observe also the correct pronunciation of "Jordan." The broad solemnity of this appeal requires the darker vowel; in brighter, lighter songs, the same river is invariably called "Jerd'n."

"Let de Heb'n-light Shine on Me" (page 76) is a good example of a slow, steady pulsation interrupted by a sudden "pause." It also shows clearly the value of the two (different) pronunciations of the word "de."

Be careful not to break the long, broad phrases with a new breath in the middle, especially after the words "way" and "brother." An interesting variation may be (for the third stanza, after the D.S.) to *hum* the first two or even three phrases, returning to the words (***pp***) to finish the song.

LET DE HEB'N-LIGHT SHINE ON ME

original key: B-flat major

Arranged by
Hall Johnson

Fine

Heb'n - light shine on me. Oh, _____

broth-er, you mus' bow so low, _____ Oh, _____ broth-er, you mus' bow so

low. _____ For low is de way to de

up-per bright worl', Let de Heb'n - light shine on me.

D.S. al Fine

MY LORD, WHAT A MORNIN'

original key

Arranged by
Hall Johnson

With mystic expectation

The musical form of this edition has been slightly adapted from Johnson's original.

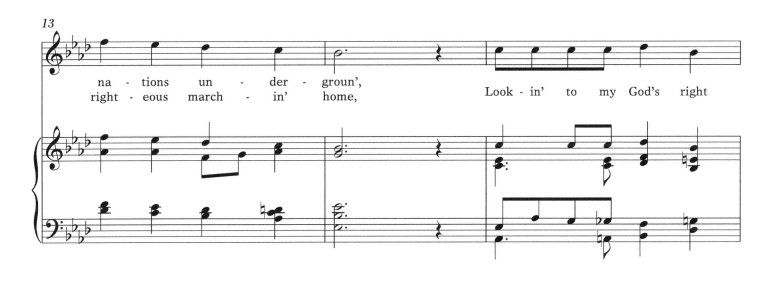

OH, GRAVEYARD

original key: F-sharp minor

Arranged by
Hall Johnson

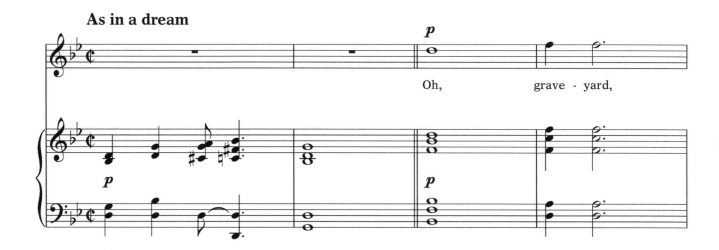

As in a dream

Oh, grave - yard,

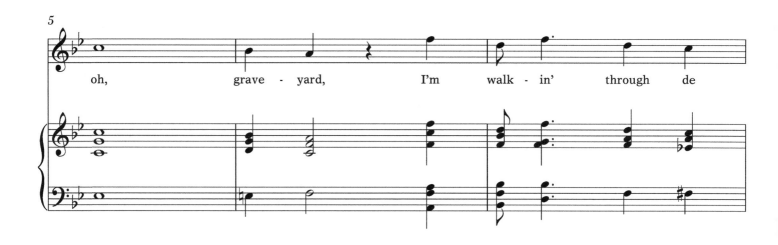

oh, grave - yard, I'm walk - in' through de

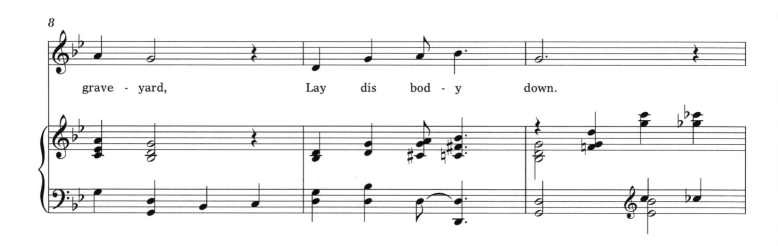

grave - yard, Lay dis bod - y down.

WERE YOU THERE?

original key

Arranged by
Hall Johnson

With changing "colors," but steady tempo

STAN' STILL, JORDAN

original key: E minor

Arranged by
Hall Johnson

brighter tempo for 3rd verse

2. You may bur - y my bod - y,_____ You may bur - y my
3. When I feel_____ de Spir - it,_____ When I feel_____ de

bod - y, You may bur - y my bod - y, But I
Spir - it, When I feel_____ de Spir - it, Lord, I

can't _____ stan' _____ still.
can't _____ stan' _____ still.

2b. (4th verse ending)

still. 4. Stan' still,_____ Jor - dan,_____

Stan' still,_____ Jor - dan, Stan' still,_____

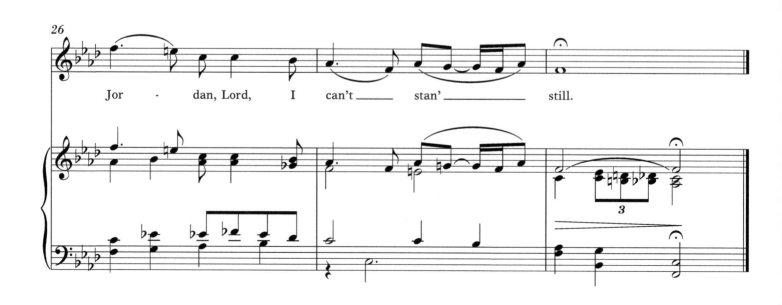

Jor - dan, Lord, I can't_____ stan'_____ still.

FAST AND BRIGHT

Hall Johnson's original introduction for the section

A slow or rapid metronome-beat will not guarantee that *every* song fitted into those beats will sound slow or fast. In any song, the impression of speed depends upon the length of the syllables and the rapidity with which they follow each other.

In this group, "Gospel Train" (page 98) and "Ev'ry Time I Feel de Spirit" (page 88) require a quick pulse with frequent accents. In the other three songs, the "beats" must be quite moderately spaced and the feeling of "brightness" supplied by crisp and vigorous enunciation of the rapid syllables.

EV'RY TIME I FEEL DE SPIRIT

original key

Arranged by
Hall Johnson

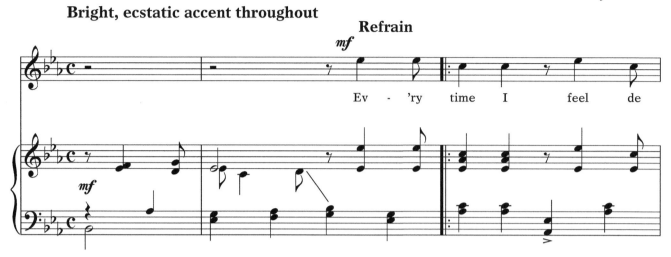

The musical form of this edition has been slightly adapted from Johnson's original.

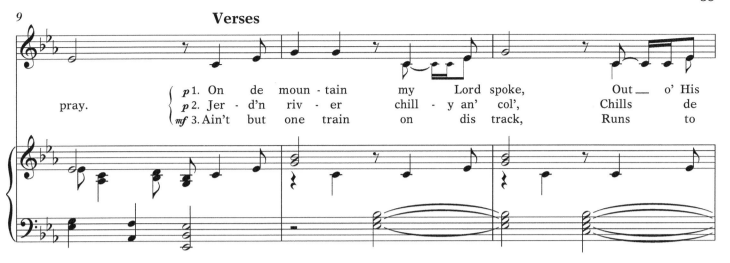

Verses

1. On de moun-tain my Lord spoke, Out o' His
2. Jer-d'n riv-er chill-y an' col', Chills de
3. Ain't but one train on dis track, Runs to

mouth came fire an' smoke. In de val-ley, on my knees, Ask' my
bod-y but not de soul. All a-roun' me look so shine, Ask' my
Heav-en an' runs right back. Saint Pe-ter wait-in' at de gate Says, "Come on,

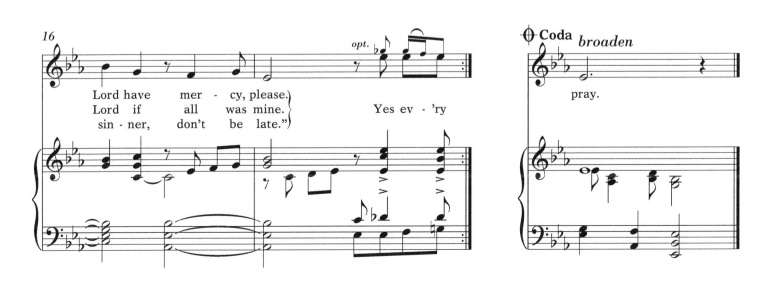

Lord have mer-cy, please.
Lord if all was mine. Yes ev-'ry
sin-ner, don't be late."

Coda *broaden*

pray.

GLORY HALLELUJAH TO DE NEW-BORN KING

Christmas Spiritual

original key

Arranged by
Hall Johnson

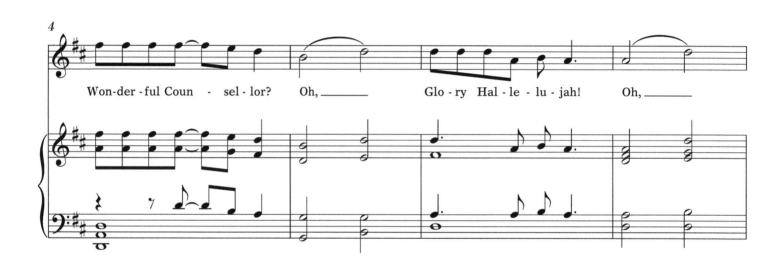

24

Glory Hal - le - lu - jah! Glo - ry Hal - le - lu - jah to de new-born King. _ You'll

27

find Him in Beth - le - hem wrapped in de man - ger, Oh, _____

30

Glo - ry Hal - le - lu - jah! Oh, _____ Glo - ry Hal - le - lu - jah!

33

Glo - ry Hal - le - lu - jah to de new-born King. _ Cry - in' "Peace on earth, _ good - will _

D.S. al Fine

RELIGION IS A FORTUNE

original key

Arranged by
Hall Johnson

Bright and happy

The musical form of this edition has been slightly adapted from Johnson's original.

WHEN I LAY MY BURDEN DOWN

original key

Arranged by
Hall Johnson

Exultant—but not too fast

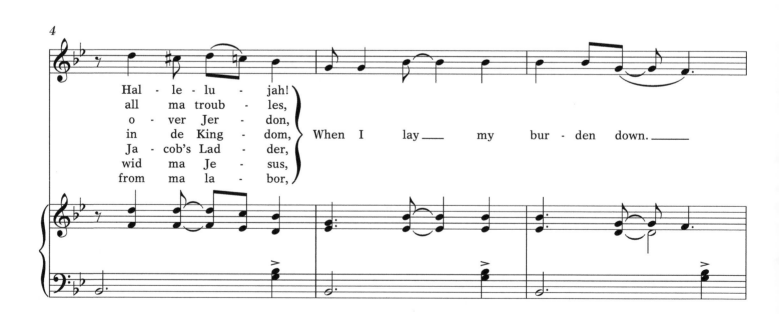

GOSPEL TRAIN

original key

Arranged by
Hall Johnson

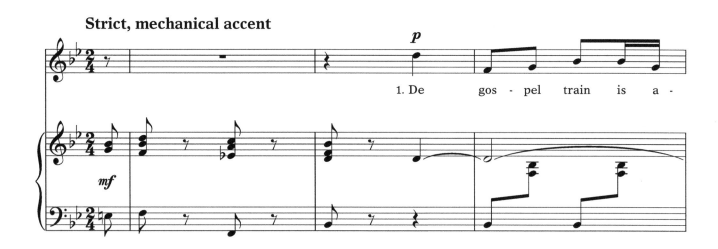

The musical form of this edition has been slightly adapted from Johnson's original.

43 Refrain

boa'd, lit - tle chil - d'n, git on boa'd, lit - tle chil - d'n, git on

47

boa'd, lit - tle chil - d'n, Dere's room for man - y - a mo'. 4. She's

51

near - in' now __ de sta - tion, Oh, sin - ner, don't be vain, __ But

55

come an' git __ yo' tick - et An' __ be read - y for __ dis train. Oh, git on